The George Washington Devotional

by Damon T. Cagle

BrightVirtue
PUBLISHING

ISBN: 978-0-9891647-9-5
First Printing 2013

Published by Bright Virtue Publishing
www.bright-virtue.com
Printed in the United States of America

TABLE OF CONTENTS

A Word to Homeschoolers:

The material in *The George Washington Devotional* was designed to be easily assimilated into a homeschool curriculum. It is suggested that the book be completed over the course of one semester. Since there are thirty-four lessons, a child completing two lessons per week will finish the book in seventeen weeks. To complete two lessons per week, the child should follow something similar to the following schedule:

Monday	Lesson 1A
Tuesday	Lesson 1B
Wednesday	Lesson 2A
Thursday	Lesson 2B
Friday	Free

Of course, the book can be done in fewer than seventeen weeks. Alternatively, it can be done more slowly. For example, to complete the book over the period of a school year the child should complete about one lesson per week. This would be done by working only two days per week on the devotional.

Reading level for the devotional is roughly second grade. However, it might also be appropriate for high-level first graders or low-level third graders. Even non-readers could benefit from the devotional by the parent reading aloud to the child and asking the questions orally.

After some thought, no testing materials have been included. The main reason for this is that the basic purpose of the devotional is not history nor biography, but spiritual growth. However, a parent might easily construct a test of the history/biography portions of the book by simply lifting questions from completed lessons.

Foreword

The George Washington Devotional is a unique way for children to discover, in a very personal way, the truths of Christ. While it may indeed be useful as a tool for history, that subject plays a secondary role to the Christian devotional. By learning about the personal achievements, failures, struggles, and eccentricities of an individual such as Washington, it is the belief of the author that a child will be able to more correctly and meaningfully apply lessons to his/her own life. Specifically, the biography element is meant to intimate to the child the life of a single person, from birth to death. The hope is that the child will be able to closely relate with the life of the subject of the biography.

The parent is an indispensable part of the learning process. The author has taken reasonable care not to make value judgments regarding the actions of the subject of the biography. Rather, emphasis is placed upon application of a particular situation to the life of the child. Moreover, the devotions are intensely introspective, with the intent of coaxing the child into personalizing situations and emotions. Thus, parents should be willing and available to discuss the material and help guide the child through this process of self-discovery and his/her discovery of the Christ.

All of the biographical information in this devotional was derived from: *Life of Washington*, Washington Irving, Kelmscott Society Pub., New York, 1855.

All verses in this devotional are taken from the *New American Standard Bible* (NASB).

LESSON 1a

WORK

George Washington was born in Virginia in 1732. Many people in George's family were soldiers. One of the soldiers in George's family was his older brother, Lawrence. Lawrence had sailed on ships and gone to places that were very far away from home.

When George was eight years old, he wanted to be a soldier like Lawrence. Sometimes, George would play games with his friends. In one of the games, his friends would pretend to be soldiers and George would be their leader. The boys would march like soldiers and put on parades in the schoolyard.

Answer these questions about the story:

1. Where was George Washington born?

   _____

2. Where were you born?

   _____

3. Who was George's brother?

   _____

4. Do you have a brother?

   _____

5. What did George want to be when he grew up?

   _____

6. What do you want to be when you grow up?

    _____

7. Do you ever pretend to be someone you're not?

    _____

    What do you pretend?

    _____

    _____

    _____

LESSON 1b

WORK

> **Verse for the day:** *My food is to do the will of Him who sent Me and to accomplish His work.*
>
> *John 4:34 (NASB)*

Remember the story you read about the kind of work George Washington wanted to do when he grew up? He wanted to be a soldier.

Someday, when you grow up, you will have a job. You might be a farmer, an actor, or a doctor. In your job, you might work by growing food, making a movie, or fixing a broken arm.

In the verse above, Jesus is talking about doing work. Jesus wanted to do work for his Father. He wanted to do God's work.

God wants you to do work for him too. He wants you to be kind to others, help others, and to love everyone you meet.

Answer these questions:

1. Whose work did Jesus want to do?

   _____

   Can you do God's work too?

   _____

2. Name three things you have done this week to work

   for God.

   _____

   _____

   _____

3. Name three things you can do today to work for

   God.

   _____

   _____

   _____

> **Prayer:** *Lord, help me work for you today. Help me to be kind to others. Help me to love everyone I meet the way that Jesus loved them. Amen.*

LESSON 2a

EDUCATION

George Washington went to a very small school when he was eight years old. It probably had only one room, and the students were all different ages. The things he learned were a lot like the things you are learning. He learned to read, write, and do math.

George's brother, Lawrence, was very lucky. He got to cross the ocean to England to go to school. The trip to England took him many days on a ship. Lawrence stayed away from home for a long time to learn everything he could. He didn't come home until he was twenty two years old!

Answer these questions about the story:

1. How many rooms did George Washington's school have?

   _____

2. Where did George's brother go to school?

   _____

3. Is your school small like George's or is it big?

   _____

4. How did George's brother get to England?

   _____

   _____

જ્જ

5. How old was George's brother when he came back from school?

_____

6. What are some things you learn in school?

_____

_____

_____

_____

∽∽

LESSON 2b

EDUCATION

Verse for the day: *And Jesus kept increasing in wisdom and stature, and in favor with God and men*
Luke 2:52 (NASB)

Remember the story you read about George Washington going to school?

All children learn things as they grow up. Most children learn these things at school. Others learn at home from their parents. Still others work with their fathers or mothers to learn how to do their parents jobs.

In the verse above, we see that Jesus learned things as he grew up too. He gained wisdom. Learning math will teach us how to add numbers, and learning science will teach us how birds fly. Learning wisdom will show us how to act toward others and to make good decisions.

We can learn wisdom several ways, but the best way is to learn it from God. God can teach us wisdom through the Bible, prayer, and by speaking to our hearts.

Answer these questions:

1. What did Jesus learn as he grew up?

   _____

2. What will wisdom help us do?

   _____

   _____

∂∽∾

3. How can we learn God's wisdom?

_____

_____

4. Name three things God has taught you to do.

_____

_____

_____

Prayer: *Lord, help me to learn your wisdom. Help me to know how to act toward others, and help me to make wise decisions. Amen.*

❦

LESSON 3a

COMMUNICATION

Many years ago, when George Washington was a boy, there were no telephones or computers. People who wanted to talk to each other had to write letters if they lived far apart. Sometimes it would take weeks for a letter to get from one place to another, especially if the letter had to go to another country.

George's brother, Lawrence, lived far away in England. Lawrence wrote letters to George and his family back in America. George enjoyed the letters. He got to hear about England and other places that Lawrence traveled. He also got to hear stories about Lawrence being a soldier. George and his family would write to Lawrence too. They would tell Lawrence what was going on at home in America.

Answer these questions about the story:

1. How did Lawrence tell his family in America about England?

   _____

2. How do you talk to your family when you are away from them?

   _____

   _____

3. How long would it take a letter to get to America from England?

   _____

4. Does it take you that long to call someone on the phone?

   _____

ॐ

5. What kinds of things did Lawrence tell about in his letters?

_____

_____

6. What do you like to talk about when you write a letter or call

someone on the telephone?

_____

_____

ᘔᘓ

LESSON 3b

COMMUNICATION

Verse for the day: *But Jesus Himself would often slip away to the wilderness and pray.*

Luke 5:16 (NASB)

Remember the story you read about George and Lawrence Washington writing letters to each other? That was the only way they had to speak to each other.

You can speak to your friends and relatives face-to-face, or you might call them on the telephone. You might even send them a text message or an email.

In the verse above, we learn that Jesus spoke with his Father too. He spoke with his Father by praying. It was so important for Jesus to have time speaking with his Father that he would go off into the wilderness so that he could be alone to pray.

We can speak with God in the same way that Jesus did. Praying is how we talk with God. We can thank Him for the things He has done for us and we can ask Him to help us when we need help. In return, He can speak with us, comfort us, or help us make good decisions.

Answer these questions:

1. How did Jesus speak with His Father?

   _____

2. Where would he go to pray?

   _____

ତ∽ତ

3. Where do you like to pray?

_____

_____

4. Name two things you could thank God for doing.

_____

_____

5. Name two things you could ask God to do.

_____

_____

Prayer: *Lord, thank you for speaking with me in prayer. Please help me to remember to pray. Help me remember to thank you for the things you have done for me. Amen.*

৯৶৶

LESSON 4a

WIDOW

When George was only eleven years old, his father died. This made George's mother a widow.

A widow is a woman whose husband has died. George's mother cared for the family by herself after that. This was especially hard because George had five younger brothers and sisters.

George's mother had a big responsibility. She had to make sure that all the children learned to read and write. She taught the children other things at home, such as good manners. George's father had left a lot of land to take care of too. Sometimes, George's older brothers helped his mother with her responsibilities.

Answer these questions about the story:

1. How old was George when his father died?

   _____

2. What is a "widow"?

   _____

   _____

3. How many younger brothers and sisters did George have?

   _____

4. What are some of the responsibilities George's mother had?

_____

_____

_____

_____

5. What are some responsibilities your parents have?

_____

_____

_____

_____

_____

LESSON 4b

WIDOW

> **Verse for the day:** *Children, obey your parents in the Lord, for this is right.*
>
> *Ephesians 6:1 (NASB)*

Remember the story you read about George Washington's mother raising the children as a widow?

George Washington's mother was left with a lot of responsibility. She had to raise all the children without a husband. Your parents have a responsibility too. They have the responsibility of raising you. This takes a lot of time, money, and effort.

In the verse above, the Bible tells us that we should obey our parents. Parents might ask us to do chores around the house to help, or they might ask us to follow certain rules. By obeying them, we help them with their responsibility of raising us.

Answer these questions:

1. Who does the verse ask us to obey?

   _____

2. What kinds of things might our parents ask us to do?

   _____

   _____

∂∞∂

3. Name three things you could do to help your parents with their
   responsibility of raising you.

   _____

   _____

   _____

Prayer: *Lord, thank you for giving me someone to help raise me. Help me to obey them, even when it's hard. Amen.*

❧❧

LESSON 5a

SPORTS

George Washington liked sports. He was bigger than most children his age. He was also very strong. He was good at running, jumping, and throwing. One story says that he threw a rock all the way across a wide river when he was just a boy. He was also good with horses, and he could ride very well. He could even control a wild horse.

Sometimes, George would have contests with his friends in wrestling or lifting heavy weights. George would win much of the time because his body was built well for those kinds of sports.

Answer these questions about the story:

1. What are some sports that George Washington could do well?

   _____

   _____

   _____

2. What are some sports that you like to play or watch?

   _____

   _____

   _____

3. Are you good at those sports?

   _____

4. Have you ever ridden a horse like George Washington?

_____

5. Can you think of any sports you do not need to be big and strong to

play well?

_____

_____

_____

_____

LESSON 5b

SPORTS

> *Verse for the day:* ...let us run with endurance the race that is set before us...
>
> *Hebrews 12:1b (NASB)*

Remember the story you read about George Washington being good at sports? Sports are fun, even if we are not as good at them as George Washington.

The verse above talks about a race, but it does not mean a foot race. The verse is talking about going through life as if it were a race. In a foot race, you have to run very hard all the way, or else you will not win. In life, we must try hard every day to follow what God wants us to do.

To be good at sports you have to have strength like George Washington. To follow God, we have to be strong too, but not in our muscles. We must be strong in our spirit.

Answer these questions:

1. Is the verse talking about a foot race? _____

2. Where do we need to be strong to help us run in life's race?

_____

ॐॐ

3. Can you think of ways to make your spirit strong so that you will have endurance for life's race?

_____

_____

_____

Prayer: *Lord, please give me strength to follow you. Help me to try my best every day for you. Amen.*

LESSON 6a

INHERITANCE

George's brother, Lawrence, was an adult when their father died. Their father left Lawrence a very good piece of land when he died. Lawrence stopped being a soldier after that and moved onto the land his father gave him. He got married and lived there with his new wife.

Many years ago, people had a habit of naming pieces of land. When Lawrence had been in the army, he had met a famous naval commander named Admiral Vernon. Lawrence named his new home "Mount Vernon," in honor of the famous commander.

Answer these questions about the story:

1. What did George's father leave to Lawrence when he died?

   _____

2. Who moved to the new piece of land with Lawrence?

   _____

3. What did Lawrence name the land?

   _____

4. Who was the land named after?

   _____

ॐॐ

5. Have you ever named something of yours, like a pet, toy, or plant?

6. _____

    If so, why did you choose the name you did?

    _____

    _____

    _____

LESSON 6b

INHERITANCE

Verse for the day: *By this all men will know that you are My disciples, if you have love for one another.*

John 13:35 (NASB)

Remember the story you read about Lawrence Washington naming Mount Vernon after a famous soldier?

If we follow Jesus, we have been named after someone too. We have been named after Jesus Christ. That is why we are called "Christians." It means that we follow Jesus' teachings. Do you see the word "Christ" in the word "Christian"?

"Disciple" means "follower". The verse above tells how people will know that we are followers of Christ. People will know because we love each other.

Answer these questions:

1. Who have we been named after if we are followers of Jesus?

   _____

2. What is the name we are called?

   _____

3. How will people know that we follow Jesus?

   _____

   _____

ॐ∽ॐ

4. Name three ways you can show other Christians that you love them?

_____

_____

_____

Prayer: *Lord, please help me to love other Christians. Help me to do things that show them that I love them. Amen.*

LESSON 7a

RESPONSIBILITY

George would often go on visits to Lawrence's house at Mount Vernon. George met new friends there. One of the people he met was Lord Fairfax. Lord Fairfax was a very rich man, and he had lots of land. In fact, he had so much land that he had never seen all of it!

When George was sixteen, Lord Fairfax gave George a job. He told George to go out and survey all of his land. That meant that George would measure the land to see how big it was. George would also have to see if the land was good for growing crops and find out if there were any people living on Lord Fairfax's land.

Answer these questions about the story:

1. Who was the rich man that George met at Mount Vernon?

    _____

2. What job did Lord Fairfax give to George?

    _____

3. Have you ever been given a job? If so, what job were you given?

    _____

    _____

4. What things was George trying to find out in the survey?

_____

_____

_____

_____

5. Do you always try to do your best when you are given a job to do?

_____

Why?

_____

_____

_____

_____

LESSON 7b

RESPONSIBILITY

> **Verse for the day:** *And he said unto them, "Go into all the world and preach the gospel to all creation."*
>
> *Mark 16:15 (NASB)*

Remember the story you read about Lord Fairfax giving a job to George Washington?

In the verse above we see that God has given us a job as well. Our job is to tell everyone God's message.

George Washington got his job when he was sixteen, but the job God gives us begins as soon as we come to know Him. Our job might begin when we are even younger than sixteen, and it goes on as long as we live!

God wants us to share his message with everyone, children and adults, whether they live next door to us or across the ocean.

Answer these questions:

1. What job has God given us?

   _____

   _____

2. When do we begin the job God has given us?

   _____

3. With whom does God want us to share his message?

_____

_____

4. Name three people with whom you can share His message?

_____

_____

_____

Prayer: _Lord, thank you for trusting me with the responsibility of sharing your message. Please help me to tell others about your love. Amen._

∾∾

LESSON 8a

PERSEVERANCE

Surveying for Lord Fairfax was not an easy job for George to do. When George went out to look at the land, he was away from home for weeks. He had to sleep outside on the ground every night, even in the rain. Some nights he slept on a bear skin, and some nights he slept on hay for the horses. One night, the hay he was sleeping on caught on fire! George was almost burned!

While he was out, George had to find his own food. He would eat wild turkeys or other animals from the woods. He would cook them with sticks over a fire that he made himself.

Answer these questions about the story:

1. Where would George have to sleep when he was surveying?

   _____

2. Have you ever slept outside on the ground?

   _____

3. Would you like to sleep outside every night?

   _____

   Why?

   _____

   _____

   _____

4. What did George eat when he was surveying?

_____

_____

5. What would you eat if you had to find your own food in the woods?

_____

_____

_____

_____

LESSON 8b

PERSEVERANCE

> **Verse for the day:** *...forgetting what lies behind and reaching forward to what lies ahead, I press on toward the goal for the prize of the upward call of God in Christ Jesus.*
>
> *Philippians 3:13b-14 (NASB)*

Remember the story you read about George Washington sleeping on the ground in the rain?

Sometimes things are not easy. You probably don't have to sleep out in the rain like George Washington, but there are things that you have to do that are hard. Sometimes you may have to eat food you don't like, do chores you don't want to do, or sit beside someone you'd rather not.

The verse above is talking about doing things that are not easy. It talks about pressing on for a prize. It is not always easy to do what God wants us to do. In fact, sometimes it is very hard. Like running a long race, we may get tired or frustrated. Still, we should try our hardest to obey God.

Answer these questions:

1. What are some things that you have to do, but that you don't like to do?

   _____

   _____

   _____

ॐॐ

2. Is following what God wants you to do always easy?

_____

3. Name three things that God wants you to do that are not easy.

_____

_____

_____

Prayer: _Lord, please forgive me when I don't do the things you want me to do. Help me to have the strength to obey you even when it is not easy. Amen._

LESSON 9a

HELPING

Lawrence became an important leader in Virginia. Though Lawrence was several years older than George, they were still good friends. Lawrence helped George in many ways. When George was old enough, Lawrence helped him get a job as a soldier. With Lawrence's help, George became an officer in the army and got to lead other soldiers.

When Lawrence was still a young man, he got very sick and died. George was only twenty years old when his brother died. Because taking care of Mount Vernon was a big chore, George helped Lawrence's wife after Lawrence died. After Lawrence's wife died too, George went to live at Mount Vernon.

Answer these questions about the story:

1. What job did Lawrence help George get?

   _____

2. Do you think George was glad to have the job?

   _____

   Why?

   _____

   _____

3. Do your brothers, sisters, or friends ever help you get something you

   want?

   _____

4. Who did George help after Lawrence died?

_____

5. What things do you help your brothers, sisters or friends do?

_____

_____

_____

6. Where did George Washington go to live after Lawrence's wife died?

_____

ᘉᘉ

LESSON 9b

HELPING

> **Verse for the day:** *With good will render service, as to the Lord, and not to men….*
>
> *Ephesians 6:7 (NASB)*

Remember the story you read about George Washington and Lawrence helping each other?

Everyone needs help sometimes. You might need help tying your shoes, fixing your bike, or cleaning your room. Wouldn't it be nice to get help whenever you need it?

The verse above talks about serving others. It says that you should serve others as if you were serving God. When others need help, God wants us to help them. When we do, it is like we are working for God. Just like you would like others to help you, others would like to have your help as well.

Answer these questions:

1. Name some things you need help doing?

   _____

   _____

   _____

2. When we help others, who are we really working for?

   _____

ᘒᘓ

3. Name three things you can do to help others today.

_____

_____

_____

Prayer: *Lord, remind me to help others. Help me remember that when I'm really working for you when I help someone else. Amen.*

∾∾

LESSON 10a

PEACE

One of the things that George Washington did as a soldier was to try to make peace with the Native-American tribes in Virginia. George would meet with the leaders and chiefs of the Native-Americans and talk to them. Making peace was an important job because a war between the Native-Americans and Virginians would cause a lot of people to be killed.

One way of making peace was to offer gifts. George Washington would offer gifts to the Native-Americans, and the Native-Americans would offer gifts to George. Sometimes this helped people become friends and live together without fighting.

Answer these questions about the story:

1. With whom did George Washington try to make peace?

   _____

2. Do you ever argue with your brothers, sisters, or friends?

   _____

3. What do you argue about?

   _____

   _____

   _____

4. In George Washington's time, what was one way people made peace?

_____

5. How do you make up with your brothers, sisters, or friends after you argue?

_____

_____

_____

_____

LESSON 10b

PEACE

Verse for the day: *Peace I leave with you; my peace I give to you…*

John 14:27a (NASB)

Remember the story you read about George Washington trying to make peace with the Native-Americans?

Peace means many different things. It can mean that two countries are not at war. It can also mean that two people are not fighting with each other. Another kind of peace is peace between man and God.

You might have a disagreement with one of your friends. If so, you might not want to talk to that person. Later, you would need to apologize and make up with them. This is how you make peace.

The verse above talks about peace. Jesus says that he left us with peace. Sin once caused us to be apart from God. Now Jesus has helped us make peace with God.

Answer these questions:

1. What causes us to be apart from God?

_____

2. What did Jesus leave us with?

_____

ॐॐ

3. Is there anyone you need to make peace with?

_____

If so, who?

_____

_____

4. Is there anything keeping you from having peace with God today?

_____

If so, what?

_____

_____

Prayer: _Lord, help me to make peace with others. Thank you for sending Jesus to make peace with me. Amen._

LESSON 11a

ADVISOR

Once, when George Washington was still a young soldier, he was marching to a battle. The army was going slowly because the road was rough and narrow. In fact, the road was so narrow that the army was stretched four miles long! The general who was leading the army was worried that they would not make it to the battle on time.

The general was from England and did not know much about Virginia. Since George Washington grew up in Virginia, the general asked him for advice. George Washington told the general to leave half the army behind with the heavy supplies. This would let the other half of the army move faster since they would not have to carry the supplies. The general followed George Washington's advice.

Answer these questions about the story:

1. Why was the army moving so slowly?

   _____

   _____

2. Why was the general worried?

   _____

   _____

3. Do you move slowly sometimes?

   _____

4. What slows you down?

_____

_____

5. Why did the general ask George Washington's advice?

_____

_____

6. Did the general follow George Washington's advice?

_____

LESSON 11b

ADVISOR

> **Verse for the day:** *...for the Holy Spirit will teach you in that very hour what you ought to say.*
>
> *Luke 12:12 (NASB)*

Remember the story you read about George Washington giving advice to the general?

Even the smartest people need advice sometimes. You might ask your parents for advice, and children younger than you might ask you for advice. Even your parents might ask their pastor, doctor, or lawyer for advice.

The verse above talks about the Holy Spirit. The Holy Spirit speaks to us and tells us what to do and what to say. The Holy Spirit can help us know the mind of God. Like a good advisor, it's important to listen to the Holy Spirit so that you will know the right thing to do.

Answer these questions:

1. Who can help us know the mind of God?

   _____

2. What kind of things might the Holy Spirit tell us?

   _____

   _____

೫೦೫

3. Name three things that you need advice for?

_____

_____

_____

4. Could the Holy Spirit help you with these things?

_____

Prayer: *Lord, thank you for sending the Holy Spirit to give me advice. Please help me follow the Holy Spirit. Amen.*

∽∽

LESSON 12a

BRAVERY

In one battle, George Washington's army was losing badly. George Washington stayed at the front of the battle to lead his men. This was very dangerous. George Washington's horse was shot while he was riding it. When he found another horse, it was shot too! Washington had four bullet holes in his clothes before the day was over. Men who had watched him on that day thought he would be killed at any moment, but he was never hurt.

Years later, George Washington met a Native-American who was on the other side of the battle. That man told George Washington that the Native-Americans had seen what he had done. They had begun a legend that George Washington could not be killed in battle.

Answer these questions about the story:

1. Why did George Washington stay at the front of the battle?

   _____

2. How many bullet holes were in his clothes at the end of the day?

   _____

3. Do you think George Washington was afraid?

   _____

4. What things are you afraid of?

   _____

   _____

   _____

5. Have you ever been brave by doing something even though you were afraid?

_____

If so, what?

_____

_____

_____

LESSON 12b

BRAVERY

> **Verse for the day:** Even though I walk through the valley of the shadow of death, I fear no evil, for You are with me; Your rod and Your staff, they comfort me.
>
> Psalms 23:4 (NASB)

Remember the story you read about George Washington being brave during the battle?

Different things make people afraid. Some children are afraid of the dark. Others are afraid of bugs or snakes. Everyone is afraid of something, even adults.

The verse above talks about walking through a scary place. Sometimes we have to face things that are scary, but God promises to be with us and to comfort us. We will never have to face scary things all by ourselves. God will always be there with us.

Answer these questions:

1. Have you ever felt alone and afraid?

_____

If so, when?

_____

_____

୭୭

2. How do your parents comfort you when you're afraid?

_____

_____

_____

3. Who has promised to comfort us when we face scary things?

_____

Prayer: *Lord, thank you for promising to be with me when I face scary things. Please help me feel you near me when I'm afraid. Amen.*

✌❧

LESSON 13a

DISCOURAGEMENT

By the time George Washington was twenty-five, he had a high rank in the army. He was a colonel, and was put in charge of many men. He helped build forts to protect the people of Virginia, and he gave his advice to leaders in the government.

Things did not go well for him all of the time, though. Sometimes his plans did not work. Sometimes the men in the government would not take his advice. Once, Washington wrote to a friend. He told his friend that he was thinking about quitting the army because he was not good at being a leader. He was thinking about going home to Mount Vernon, but he did not. He stayed in the army and kept trying to protect the people of Virginia.

Answer these questions about the story:

1. What did George Washington help build to protect Virginia?

   _____

2. What did Washington tell his friend that he was thinking of doing?

   _____

3. Why was Washington thinking about quitting the army?

   _____

   _____

   _____

4. Have you ever thought you were not very good at something?

_____

If so, what were you not very good at?

_____

_____

_____

Did you quit doing it?

_____

Why?

_____

_____

_____

⚮

LESSON 13b

DISCOURAGMENT

Verse for the day: *Therefore, my beloved brethren, be steadfast, immovable, always abounding in the work of the Lord, knowing that your toil is not in vain in the Lord.*

I Corinthians 15:58 (NASB)

Remember the story you read about George Washington thinking of leaving the army?

Like George Washington, we sometimes get frustrated at things. If you get way behind in a game or think a job is too hard, you might feel like quitting.

God wants us to keep on working for Him, even when we feel like things will not work out. The verse above talks about being steadfast. "Steadfast" means that something doesn't change easily. God does not want us to change by stopping His work. He wants us to go on, though it may be hard. He promises that our work will pay off in the end.

Answer these questions:

1. What does "steadfast" mean?

_____

_____

2. What does God want us to keep doing?

_____

_____

∽∽

3. What does God promise about our work for Him?

_____

_____

4. What things make you want to quit working for God sometimes?

_____

_____

_____

Prayer: *Lord, please give me the strength to be steadfast in your work. Help me overcome the things that get in my way when I'm working for you. Amen.*

ᔕᔕ

LESSON 14a

MARRIAGE

One day while George Washington was on a mission, he met a man on a ferryboat crossing the river. The man invited him to dinner. Although he was in a hurry, George Washington went to the man's house for dinner. While he was there, he met a young widow named Martha. Martha had two small children at home. George and Martha talked and found out that they liked each other. They decided that they would get married as soon as they could. Once they were married, they made their home at Mount Vernon.

Answer these questions about the story:

1. Where did George Washington meet the man who invited him to

   dinner? _____

2. What was the name of the young widow he met?

   _____

3. What did George and Martha decide to do?

   _____

4. Where did they live together?

   _____

5. Do you know where your parents met?

   _____

౩ఆ

If you said "no" in question 5, ask your parents where they met.

Where did they meet?

_____

_____

6. Where would you like to live when you grow up?

_____

_____

_____

LESSON 14b

MARRIAGE

> **Verse for the day:** *...in whom you are also being built together into a dwelling of God in the Spirit.*
>
> *Ephesians 2:22 (NASB)*

Remember the story you read about George Washington and Martha deciding to marry?

Marriage is a decision to build your life with another person. It requires hard work and cooperation by both people. It's a special relationship that puts two people together for life.

God puts Christians together as well. He is building us into His Church. His Church is not a building, but a group of people who love Him. Just as in a marriage, each person will have to work hard and cooperate to make the Church into what God wants it to be. The verse above reminds us that God is building us together just like bricks are built into a house.

Answer these questions:

1. Who is putting Christians together to build the Church?

   _____

2. What does the verse say that God is building us into?

   _____

⮞⮜

3. What do you think it means that we are God's dwelling?

_____

_____

_____

4. Name three things you can do to help make the Church into what God wants it to be.

_____

_____

_____

Prayer: *Lord, thank you for giving me other Christians to work with. Help me to cooperate with them and do my part in your work. Amen.*

LESSON 15a

MODESTY

George Washington took a break from being a soldier. He was elected to be a lawmaker in Virginia. When he was introduced to the other lawmakers, a man gave a speech about Washington. The man told the other lawmakers how great a soldier Washington was and thanked him for serving the people of Virginia.

When the man had finished, George Washington wanted to speak too, but he was embarrassed by all the good things the man had said about him. When he stood up to talk, he blushed and stuttered. The man told George Washington to sit back down. He then told the other lawmakers that, on top of being a good soldier, Washington was also very modest.

Answer these questions about the story:

1. What was George Washington elected to be in Virginia?

   _____

2. What happened to George Washington when he stood up to talk?

   _____

   _____

3. How do you feel when other people say good things about you?

   _____

   _____

4. What embarrasses you?

_____

_____

5. Look up the word "modest" in the dictionary. What does it mean?

_____

_____

_____

LESSON 15b

MODESTY

> **Verse for the day:** *Humble yourselves in the presence of the Lord, and He will exalt you.*
>
> *James 4:10 (NASB)*

Remember the story you read about George Washington being modest?

When someone gives you a complement how do you react? Do you thank them or do you blush? Each person has things that he or she does well. Some people play sports well. Others are good at math or cooking.

It's okay to be good at something, but we must be careful not to become proud. "Humble" is another word for modest. In the verse above we see that God wants us to be humble. He wants us to be humble about the things that we do well. He also wants us to be humble about our faith. We should not make others feel lower than us.

Others may think we are good at something or bad at something. What they think is not so important. We shouldn't be interested in what others think of us, but instead what God thinks of us.

Answer these questions:

1. What are some things you do well?

_____

_____

_____

2. What do you do when people tell you that you are good at those

    things?

    _____

    _____

3. Who should we try to impress, God or other people?

    _____

> **Prayer:** *Lord, help me to be humble. Help me not to make others feel small. Let me try to impress you instead of trying to impress others. Amen.*

∽∽

LESSON 16a

GUARDIAN

Martha already had two children when George Washington married her. She had a boy who was six, and a girl who was four. The children's father had left a lot of money and land when he died. George Washington took care of the money and land for the children.

George and Martha never had any more children. George helped Martha raise the boy and girl. He treated them like his own children and helped teach them manners and many other things.

Answer these questions about the story:

1. How many children did Martha have when she married George?

   _____

2. What did the children's father leave them when he died?

   _____

3. Did George and Martha have any children together?

   _____

4. Who raises you?

   _____

5. Do you know anyone who is raised by someone other than their parents?

   _____

෯෬

If so, who raises them?

_____

_____

LESSON 16b

GUARDIAN

> **Verse for the day:** *"And I will be a father to you, and you shall be sons and daughters to Me," says the Lord Almighty.*
>
> *II Corinthians 6:18 (NASB)*

Remember the story you read about George Washington raising Martha's children? George Washington treated the children as if they were his own, even though he was not their father.

In the same way, God takes us in and treats us as if we were His own children. He acts like a father to us. Your parents love you, protect you, and give you the things you need to live. God does these things for you too. He loves you, protects you, and gives you things you need. In fact, He loves you even more than your parents love you!

Answer these questions:

1. Who has taken us in as if we were His children?

   _____

2. What are some things your parents do for you?

   _____

   _____

   _____

☙❧

3. What are some things God does to show you that he loves you like a son or daughter?

_____

_____

_____

4. Do your parents give you everything you ask for?

_____

5. Does God give you everything you ask for?

_____

Why do you think that is?

_____

_____

_____

Prayer: _Lord, thank you for loving me like your own child. Please help me to learn from you, just like I learn from my parents. Amen._

LESSON 17a

WORRY

In the time of George Washington, America was still ruled by Britain. Britain had passed some laws that made the Americans angry. Many people feared they would have to go to war. A meeting of leaders from all the colonies was called. The meeting was called the Continental Congress. Two of the leaders who went from Virginia were George Washington and Patrick Henry. They met at Mount Vernon and rode their horses to the meeting together.

Britain

After meeting for only one day, all of the leaders heard that the city of Boston had been attacked by Britain. The next morning, all the leaders were worried. They began that day's meeting by reading a Psalm from the Bible. The Psalm seemed to make everyone at the meeting feel better.

Answer these questions about the story:

1. What country ruled America in Washington's time?

   _____

2. Who went to the meeting from Virginia?

   _____

   _____

3. Why were the leaders worried?

   _____

   _____

4. Do you ever get worried?

_____

5. What worries you?

_____

_____

6. What did the leaders do that made them feel better?

_____

_____

LESSON 17b

WORRY

> **Verse for the day:** *This is my comfort in my affliction, that Your word has revived me.*
>
> *Psalms 119:50 (NASB)*

Remember the story you read about the leaders feeling better after reading a Psalm?

People worry about many things. Some worry about whether they will have enough money to buy food. Others worry about being sick or hurt. Some worries are silly, like what color shirt you will wear to school or what brand of cereal you will eat in the morning.

When we worry, we may need someone or something to make us feel better. God wants to comfort us and help us not to worry. As we learned in the story about George Washington, and in the verse above, reading the Bible is one thing that helps make us feel better when we are worried. It reminds us that God is looking out for us, even when we cannot look out for ourselves. This is one way that God comforts us.

Answer these questions:

1. What are some silly worries that you have had?

_____

_____

_____

ॐॐ

2. What does the verse above say we might do to feel better when we are worried?

    _____

    _____

3. How often do you read the Bible?

    _____

4. Can you think of other ways that God can make you feel better when you are worried?

    _____

    _____

    _____

Prayer: *Lord, thank you for giving us the Bible. Please comfort me and help me feel better when I get worried. Amen.*

∽∽

LESSON 18a

WAR

When they came back to Virginia from the Continental Congress, George Washington and Patrick Henry met with other Virginia leaders. They were trying to decide whether to go to war with Britain.

Patrick Henry was a very good speaker. He was young, loud and daring. When he spoke he made some people very angry. Washington was quieter and more thoughtful. Patrick Henry made a speech to the leaders of Virginia. He told them that it was time to go to war with England. George Washington agreed with him. Since he had been a soldier, it was George Washington's job to help prepare the Virginians for battle.

Answer these questions about the story:

1. What were the leaders trying to decide?

   _____

   _____

2. Who made the speech?

   _____

3. Have you ever spoken in front of a lot of people?

   _____

~

4. Did George Washington and Patrick Henry agree that it was time for war?

   _____

5. What could George Washington do to help?

   _____

   _____

6. Talk to your parents about this lesson. Ask them if there is a time when it is all right to fight. What did they say? Is it ever alright to fight?

   _____

   _____

   _____

7. What are some things that it is <u>NOT</u> alright to fight about?

   _____

   _____

   _____

LESSON 18b

WAR

> **Verse for the day:** And the tempter came and said to Him, "If You are the Son of God, command that these stones become bread."
>
> Matthew 4:3 (NASB)

Remember the story you read about George Washington saying that it was time to go to war? Wars are almost always very long, with many battles. They are hard for the people who fight.

The verse above talks about Jesus being tempted. If you know the story the verse comes from, you know that Jesus fought temptation by using verses from the Bible. Jesus knew the things that God wanted, and He used those things to fight temptation.

Like fighting in a war, we are always fighting the temptation to sin. It is not just one battle, it is a long process with many battles, and it is not easy for us to win. Like Jesus, we can use what we know God wants to help us fight temptation.

Answer these questions:

1. Who was being tempted in the verse above?

   _____

2. What did He use to fight the temptation?

   _____

   _____

∂∽

3. How is our fight with temptation like a war?

_____

_____

_____

4. How do you learn things about God so that you can use them to fight

temptation?

_____

_____

Prayer: _Lord, help me to learn more about you. Help me to fight temptation every day. Help me remember that it will not be easy to win, but that I can win with your help. Amen._

❦❦

LESSON 19a

LEADER

Men from all over America were forming an army to fight the British. Because America had never had an army like this before, there was a lot of disagreement about who would lead it. Most of the men in the army were from the north. People in the south felt left out. They did not want the leader of the army to be from the north. They wanted someone from the south to lead the army.

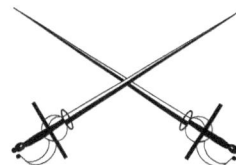

Some people said that General Lee should lead the army. He was a good soldier, but he was not born in America. Many people wanted to choose someone who was born in America. In the end, George Washington was chosen to lead the army. He was from Virginia, which is in the south, and he was born in America.

Answer these questions about the story:

1. Why didn't people in the south want a leader from the north?

   _____

   _____

2. Why wasn't General Lee chosen to lead the army?

   _____

   _____

3. Who was chosen as leader of the new army?

   _____

∼∽

4. Have you ever been chosen to lead something?

   _____

5. What kinds of things would you be good at leading?

   _____

   _____

   _____

6. What about you would make people want to choose you as a leader?

   _____

   _____

   _____

LESSON 19b

LEADER

Verse for the day: *"Where is He who has been born King of the Jews? For we saw His star in the east and have come to worship Him."*

Matthew 2:2 (NASB)

Remember the story you read about George Washington being chosen as leader of the American army?

We have all kinds of leaders. Some leaders lead armies, like George Washington. Others lead governments, businesses, or churches. Football and baseball teams have leaders too. The leader shows everyone how to behave and what to do to be successful.

The verse above is talking about the men from the east who came looking for Jesus when he was born. They were looking for a leader, a king. Jesus is our friend, but it's important to remember that Jesus is also our leader. He shows us how to behave and what to do.

Answer these questions:

1. Name three leaders you can think of and the things that they lead.

_____

_____

_____

2. As Christians, who is our leader?

_____

ॐॐ

3. Why do we need a leader?

_____

_____

4. What are some ways you can know what Jesus wants you to do?

_____

_____

_____

Prayer: _Lord, thank you for being my leader._
Help me to behave like you and to do the
things you want me to do. Amen.

✍✍

LESSON 20a

CHARITY

The army was at Boston when George Washington arrived to command it. He knew that he would be away from home for a long time, probably years. Other people would have to take care of Mount Vernon while he was gone.

George Washington was a rich man. He had lots of land and money. He knew that wars can cause many people to go without food and clothing. He sent word back home to the people who were taking care of Mount Vernon that they should never send anyone away from his home without being fed. He also said that they should give some of his money to the poor every year while he was away.

Answer these questions about the story:

1. Where was the army when Washington arrived?

   _____

2. What did Washington tell the people who were taking care of Mount Vernon to do if someone came who was hungry?

   _____

   _____

3. What did he tell them to give to the poor every year?

   _____

4. Have you ever given something to someone who needed it?

   _____

   What did you give them?

   _____

   _____

5. Has anyone ever given you something when you needed it?

   _____

ॐॐ

LESSON 20b

CHARITY

> **Verse for the day:** But whoever has the world's goods, and sees his brother in need and closes his heart against him, how does the love of God abide in him?
>
> I John 3:17 (NASB)

Remember the story you read about George Washington asking that some of his money be given to the poor?

Everyone will be in need sometime. Poor people may need money for food and clothes. Even rich people need things that their money cannot buy, like friendship and love.

The verse above shows us that if God's love is in us, we will want to help others who are in need. We can do this by giving things we have. We can give money to people who cannot buy the things they need to live. We can give time by going to visit people who are old, sick, or hurt. By doing these things, we show other people the love of God that is in our hearts.

Answer these questions:

1. What are some things that poor people may not be able to buy?

_____

_____

_____

❧❧

2. What are some things that rich people may not have that money cannot buy for them?

_____

_____

_____

3. How does the verse say that we can show people the love of God in us?

_____

_____

4. What are some things you have that you could give to those in need?

_____

_____

> **Prayer:**   *Lord, please help me to give to others. Help me show others that your love is in me. Show me the things that I have that I can give. Amen.*

LESSON 21a

HOMESICKNESS

Many of the men in the American army were not really soldiers. They were just regular people, mostly farmers who had come to help fight the British. Most of them did not have uniforms like the British, and they had never been trained on how to fight in a war.

Winter in the army was very hard. It was very cold, and there was not much food or any place to get warm. They had not yet really won a battle, and they were homesick and tired. Many of the men left the army and went home. They did not want to fight anymore. As time went on, George Washington's army got smaller and smaller as men went back home.

Answer these questions about the story:

1. How was the American army different from the English army?

   _____

   _____

   _____

2. Why was winter in the army so hard?

   _____

   _____

   _____

3. Is the winter cold where you live?

   _____

   Where you live, would it be hard to sleep in a tent in the winter?

   _____

4. Where did many of the men in Washington's army go?

   _____

   Have you ever been away from home for a long time?

   _____

   Did you want to go home when you were there?

   _____

5. What makes your home a good place to be?

   _____

   _____

   _____

LESSON 21b

HOMESICKNESS

Verse for the day: *By faith Noah, being warned by God about things not yet seen, in reverence prepared an ark for the salvation of his household…*

Hebrews 11:7a (NASB)

Remember the story you read about George Washington's army getting smaller and smaller because soldiers were leaving for home?

Have you ever had a hard job to do? Doesn't the job seem easier if someone else is there with you? Doing hard things gets even harder when you are doing them alone.

Following God is not easy. Like in George Washington's army, many people will give up. In Noah's time, he was the only person who found favor with God. There was no one else in the whole world that followed God! But, in the end, Noah and his family were the only ones saved from the flood. Few people end up really following God, but if you do He will take care of you.

Answer these questions:

1. What is a hard job that you had to do alone?

_____

_____

2. How do you feel when people around you are giving up?

_____

_____

୭ଚ

3. Who did God save from the flood?

_____

4. Why did God save him?

_____

5. Do you think you can follow God like Noah, even if you're the only

one?

_____

Prayer: _Lord, help me to follow you, even if I'm all alone. Please watch over me when no one else is there to help. Amen._

LESSON 22a

SURPRISE

The British had hired some soldiers to help them fight the Americans. These soldiers were called Hessians.

In the middle of the winter, George Washington decided to make an attack on the Hessians at Trenton. To do this, he had to cross a big river at night with thousands of men. The river was cold and icy. It was so cold that two men died that night just from the weather.

George Washington knew he would have to be smart to win the battle, but he had a plan. He would surprise the Hessians by attacking at a time when they did not think he would. He crossed the river on Christmas Eve while the Hessians were sleeping, and attacked Trenton before the Hessian soldiers got out of bed on Christmas morning. The surprise attack worked and Washington won the battle.

Answer these questions about the story:

1. Who had the English hired to help them fight the Americans?

   _____

2. What did George Washington have to do to get to Trenton?

   _____

3. What was Washington's plan?

   _____

   _____

4. Did the plan work?

   _____

5. Have you ever made a plan for doing something?

   _____

6. What was your plan?

   _____

   _____

   _____

   _____

7. Tell about a time when you were surprised by something.

   _____

   _____

   _____

LESSON 22b

SURPRISE

> **Verse for the day:** *Who does great things, unfathomable, And wondrous works without number.*
>
> *Job 9:10 (NASB)*

Remember the story you read about how George Washington's plan to surprise the Hessians worked?

Planning always pays off. If you are going to have a party, you need to plan. You have to know what games you will play, what kind of food you will eat, how to decorate, and who to invite. If you plan well, the party will be a success.

God's plan is more amazing than anything humans can imagine. The way animals, plants, air, and water all work together to make the earth a good place to live is a part of God's plan for creation. You are a part of that plan too! God planned to make you just like you are for a special purpose.

Answer these questions:

1. What kinds of things would you need to plan if you were going to go on a vacation?

   _____

   _____

   _____

ॐॐ

2. God made you just the way you are. What are some special things about you?

_____

_____

_____

3. The Bible verse above talks about someone doing "great things" and "wondrous works." Who do you think it means will do these things?

_____

Prayer: *Lord, thank you for planning for me to be a part of the world. Thank you for making me special. Help me to remember that you plan many great things. Amen.*

LESSON 23a

FOREBEARANCE

Once during the war, a letter came to George Washington. He thought the letter was written to him, but it wasn't. It was written by one of his soldiers and it was meant to go to someone else. Without noticing that the letter was not his, Washington opened the letter and read it. The soldier had said many bad things about Washington in the letter.

Washington had to decide what to do. He could have punished the soldier for writing bad things about him, but he didn't. Instead, he put the letter back in the envelope and wrote a note on it. The note said that he had opened the letter by mistake and that he was sorry for reading the soldier's private mail.

Answer these questions about the story:

1. Why did George Washington open the letter?

   _____

   _____

2. Have you ever read something private that was not yours?

   _____

3. What could Washington have done to the soldier?

   _____

   _____

4. What did Washington do when he found out that the letter was not to him?

_____

_____

_____

5. How do you think the soldier felt when he read Washington's note?

_____

_____

6. Has anyone ever said bad things about you?

_____

What did you do after they said the bad things?

_____

_____

_____

LESSON 23b

FOREBEARANCE

Verse for the day: *For of His fullness we have all received, and grace upon grace.*

John 1:16 (NASB)

Remember the story you read about how George Washington did not punish the soldier who wrote bad things about him in the letter?

Very often, someone does something that makes us angry. They might cut in line or call someone a bad name. That may make you want to quit talking to them or stay away from them. It may even make you want to do something bad to them in return.

When we sin, we are doing something which makes God angry. Every one of us has sinned at some time. We will probably sin a lot more too. Isn't it wonderful that, because of Jesus, God forgets our sins? He acts toward us as if we had never committed the sin.

Answer these questions:

1. What kinds of things do people do to make you angry?

_____

_____

_____

2. Are you able to act kind, even when someone has done wrong to you?

_____

∾∾

3. What things have you done to make God angry?

_____

_____

_____

4. Are you sorry you did these things?

_____

Prayer: _Lord, please forgive me of the sins I have done against you. Help me to show kindness to others, even if they do bad things to me. Amen._

LESSON 24a

PUNISHMENT

In one battle, George Washington had sent General Lee to the front with some soldiers. He had told General Lee to fight the British if he found them. Later, some of the soldiers came running back from the front, even though there had not been a battle yet. When George Washington went to check, he found that General Lee had ordered all of his men to retreat.

This made Washington very angry because General Lee had disobeyed him. Washington put General Lee on trial for disobeying his orders. General Lee lost the trial, and was removed from command.

Answer these questions about the story:

1. Who led the soldiers who went to the front?

   _____

2. Why were the men leaving the front?

   _____

   _____

3. Why was Washington angry?

   _____

   _____

4. Do you sometimes make your parents angry?

   _____

5. What do you do that makes them angry?

   _____

   _____

   _____

6. What did George Washington do to General Lee for disobeying his

   orders?

   _____

   _____

⤬⤬

LESSON 24b

PUNISHMENT

> **Verse for the day:** *For he who does wrong will receive the consequences of the wrong which he has done, and that without partiality.*
>
> *Colossians 3:25 (NASB)*

Remember the story you read about General Lee being punished for disobeying George Washington's orders?

Although we should always obey our parents, we do not always do it. When we do disobey, we might get punished. Did you know that something worse than punishment might happen to you if you disobey? What would happen if you disobeyed your parents by going into a busy road or putting your hand on a hot stove? The Bible teaches us that consequences will follow when we disobey, and the consequences may be worse than any punishment our parents could give us.

Answer these questions:

1. What are some rules in your house?

_____

_____

_____

⮧⮧

2. What punishment do you get if you break the rules?

   _____

   _____

   _____

3. What are some consequences that might happen if you break the rules, other than getting punished?

   _____

   _____

   _____

4. Other than your parents, who are some people you are expected to obey?

   _____

   _____

   _____

Prayer: *Lord, help me to remember that if I do wrong, consequences will follow. Help me to have a heart that wants to obey you and my parents. Amen.*

❧❦

LESSON 25a

COOPERATION

The Americans needed help to fight the British. America got help from France. The French sent ships and men to help fight. This was important because the Americans did not have a navy.

George Washington became very good friends with one of the French leaders named Lafayette. Even after the war was over, Washington and Lafayette would write letters to each other. The last big battle of the war was at Yorktown, Virginia. George Washington led the Americans into battle with the help of the French. Together, they won the battle. America would not be ruled by Britain anymore.

Answer these questions about the story:

1. Who helped the Americans fight the British?

   _____

2. How did the French help the Americans?

   _____

3. What was the name of George Washington's friend from France?

   _____

4. Where was the last big battle of the war?

   _____

5. Who led the Americans into the battle?

_____

6. What kinds of things do you need help doing?

_____

_____

_____

7. Have you ever made a friend who was not an American?

_____

If so, where was your friend from?

_____

LESSON 25b

COOPERATION

Verse for the day: *Owe nothing to anyone except to love one another; for he who loves his neighbor has fulfilled the law.*

Romans 13:8 (NASB)

Remember the story you read about Lafayette and the French helping George Washington in the war?

You probably have a lot of rules to follow in your home and at school. Rules tell us how to behave. Rules help us get along with our parents, friends, brothers, and sisters.

Wouldn't it be nice if we had just one rule to follow? The verse above shows us that if we love those around us we will be obeying all of God's rules! We will always be acting right if we show love to one another.

Answer these questions:

1. Name three people who make rules you must follow?

_____

_____

_____

2. Why do we have rules?

_____

_____

❧❧

3. How does the verse say that we can be sure we are following all of God's rules?

_____

_____

4. Name three things you can do to show those around you that you love them?

_____

_____

_____

Prayer: _Lord, thank you for giving me this rule to live by. Help me to show others every day that I love them. Amen._

❦❦

LESSON 26a

RENEWAL

When the war was over, George Washington went back home to Mount Vernon. While he was away, the buildings and farms had not been kept up like they would have if he had been home. He repaired the buildings and built a few new ones. He raised hunting dogs and horses and went fox hunting. He also planted crops in the fields.

He was glad to be home and told some of his friends that he was tired of being a soldier. He stayed at home with Martha and rested. Sometimes his friends would come to visit. Lafayette came all the way from France and stayed at Mount Vernon for two weeks.

Answer these questions about the story:

1. Where did George Washington go after the war was over?

   _____

2. What did Washington do when he got home?

   _____

   _____

3. Have you ever tried to fix anything that was broken?

   _____

   Were you able to fix it?

   _____

∾❦

4. Who came to visit George Washington?

_____

5. What do you like to do to relax?

_____

_____

_____

❦❧

LESSON 26b

RENEWAL

Verse for the day: *Come to Me, all who are weary and heavy-laden, and I will give you rest.*

Matthew 11:28 (NASB)

Remember the story you read about George Washington going home after the war?

Hard work makes people tired. They may need to go home and take a nap. They may even need to take a vacation to get rested up.

Work isn't the only thing that makes us tired. Worry has a way of making us tired, too. It can wear on us like hard work. We might get worried about school. We might get worried about an argument with our friend or parents. These things can tire us out. The verse above tells us that God can give us rest from our sins and our worries. Like a nice shade tree in the hot sun, He is a place we can go to take a break from our worries.

Answer these questions:

1. What are some things you do that make your body tired?

_____

_____

_____

2. What are some things you do to rest your body?

_____

_____

_____

3. What are some things you worry about?

_____

_____

_____

4. What does the verse say that God will give us if we come to Him?

_____

Prayer: *Lord, thank you for being a place I can go to rest. Help me to remember to come to you when I am tired or worried. Amen.*

∽∽

LESSON 27a

FIRST PRESIDENT

The Americans formed a new country made up of all the states like Virginia. It was called the United States of America. Men voted on who would be the new president. This person would be the first President of the United States. They chose George Washington.

Washington left Mount Vernon again. He went to New York to be sworn in as president. There were many people there. There were ships on the river and lots of decorations. The people watched as George Washington put his hand on the Bible and promised to keep the laws of the United States. When he finished, the man who led the oath yelled, "Long live George Washington, President of the United States!"

Answer these questions about the story:

1. What is the name of the country the Americans formed?

   _____

2. Who was chosen to be the first president?

   _____

3. What did George Washington promise to do?

   _____

   _____

∽∽

4. Have you ever been the first person to do something?

_____

If so, what did you do?

_____

_____

_____

How did you feel when you were first?

_____

Why did you feel that way?

_____

_____

_____

✍✍

LESSON 27b

FIRST PRESIDENT

> **Verse for the day:** *and behold, a voice out of the heavens said, "This is my beloved Son, in whom I am well-pleased."*
>
> *Matthew 3:17 (NASB)*

Remember the story you read about George Washington becoming the first President of the United States?

Have you ever listened to anyone make an announcement? Usually, everyone stops to listen carefully. When George Washington was announced to the crowd, everyone cheered. This was a time for the people of the country to stop and recognize an important moment, one that they would remember for the rest of their lives.

In the verse above, God made an important announcement. He announced that Jesus was his Son. God also announced that Jesus pleased Him. All the people there heard that something had happened which had never happened before. God had sent His own Son to the earth!

Answer these questions:

1. Where are some places you might hear an announcement?

_____

_____

∺ó

2. Have you ever heard something, maybe on television or on the internet, which was very important?

_____

What was it?

_____

_____

3. What was God's announcement in the verse above?

_____

_____

4. Why was that announcement so important?

_____

_____

Prayer: *Lord, thank you for sending Jesus to the earth. Help me to remember how important it is that you sent Him. Amen.*

ⷭⸯⷭ

LESSON 28a

MODEL FOR FUTURE

Since there had never been a president before, deciding how to do even little things was hard. For example, who could come to visit the president? When could they come? Could the president invite his friends over, or could he only visit with other leaders? Who would sit at the president's table at dinner?

At first, there were no rules about visitors at all. People George Washington did not even know would come just to visit him. They came all day long, every day. This made George Washington tired, and it did not leave him time to even respond to important letters. He had to make some rules about who could come to his house and when they could come.

Answer these questions about the story:

1. When he first became president, how often did George Washington have visitors?

   _____

   _____

2. How often do you have visitors?

   _____

   _____

3. Why was it a problem for George Washington to have so many visitors?

_____

_____

_____

4. What did George Washington do to solve the problem?

_____

_____

_____

✑✑

LESSON 28b

MODEL FOR FUTURE

Verse for the day: *...so that He would be the firstborn among many brethren.*

Romans 8:29b (NASB)

Remember the story you read about George Washington having to make rules for visitors?

Since George Washington was the first president, other presidents would follow what George Washington had started. George Washington was like an example for them to follow. It was easier for later presidents to know what to do because someone had already gone first.

In the same way, Jesus has gone before us to be an example to us. The verse above calls Him the "firstborn" of many brethren. It is as if He were our older brother. We can look to Him to be our example of how to behave and what kinds of things we will have to go through. Life is better because we have an example to follow.

Answer these questions:

1. What do you want to be when you grow up?

   _____

   _____

≈≈

2. Do you know a person who is an example of what you want to be when you grow up?

_____

If so, who?

_____

Who does the verse say is our Christian example?

_____

3. Name three things Jesus did, that you need to do as well.

_____

_____

_____

Prayer: *Lord, thank you for sending Jesus ahead of us to be our example. Help me to follow Jesus' example. Amen.*

✎✎

LESSON 29a

GRATEFULNESS

George Washington's friend, Lafayette, had gone back home to France. Lafayette helped lead the French people in a war against their rulers, just as he had helped Washington fight the British. The leaders that Lafayette fought had put many people in a prison called the Bastille. All the people hated the Bastille because of all the horrible things that had happened there. The French people won the war against those leaders, with the help of Lafayette.

Lafayette sent a message to George Washington, telling Washington that the French people had won the war and they were going to destroy the Bastille. With the message, Lafayette sent George Washington a gift from the French people. It was the key to the Bastille. Today, it still hangs on the wall where George Washington hung it at Mount Vernon.

Answer these questions about the story:

1. Where did Lafayette fight after he left America?

   _____

2. What was the name of the prison that the French people hated?

   _____

3. What gift did Lafayette give to Washington after the French won the war?

   _____

4. Why do you think Lafayette was so grateful to Washington?

_____

_____

_____

5. Have you ever gotten a special gift from a close friend or relative?

_____

Why was the gift so special to you?

_____

_____

_____

LESSON 29b

GRATEFULLNESS

> **Verse for the day:** *I will praise the name of God with song and magnify Him with thanksgiving.*
>
> Psalm 69:30 (NASB)

Remember the story you read about Lafayette giving George Washington a gift to thank him?

When someone does something good for us, it is nice to thank them. No doubt, Lafayette looked up to George Washington like a father. He appreciated what Washington had taught him.

In the same way, we should be thankful to God, our Father. He has taught us many things, and we should show Him our thanks. We see one way to thank God in the verse above. We can thank God by praises and singing. God will hear our praises and songs and know that we are thankful.

Answer these questions:

1. What do you do to show thanks to others?

_____

_____

_____

2. What does the verse say you can do to show thanks to God?

_____

_____

৵৵

3. What are some songs that you might sing to show God thanks?

_____

_____

_____

4. What are some things you could say to God to praise Him?

_____

_____

_____

Prayer: *Lord, thank you for teaching me how to live. Help me to remember to thank you with songs and praises. Amen.*

LESSON 30a

FAREWELL

George Washington served two terms as President of the United States, eight years in all. After that, he decided not to run for president again. He was older and was sick a lot. People in the government argued with each other all during his time as president. This made him tired of serving as president. He was ready to go home to Mount Vernon. He told a friend that he hoped never to go more than twenty miles from home again.

On his last day as president, he had a small dinner party. John Adams and Thomas Jefferson were there, both of whom would later be President of the United States. Washington told them goodbye and wished them happiness.

Answer these questions about the story:

1. How long was George Washington President of the United States?

   _____

2. What did he do on his last day as president?

   _____

   _____

   _____

3. Who was at the party?

   _____

   _____

4. Have you ever had to say goodbye to a friend that you might never see again?

_____

If so, how did you feel?

_____

_____

_____

5. Do you know anyone who has retired from work?

_____

What do they do now?

_____

_____

_____

ᘒᘒ

LESSON 30b

FAREWELL

> **Verse for the day:** *If I go and prepare a place for you, I will come again and receive you to Myself, that where I am, there you may be also.*
>
> *John 14:3 (NASB)*

Remember the story you read about George Washington saying goodbye to his friends when he left the presidency?

You might have to say goodbye to a friend who is moving, or you might have to say goodbye to your grandparents after a visit. Saying goodbye can be hard if you know you may not see the person again for a long time.

On the night before Jesus died, He met with His disciples. He knew that He would not see them again on earth. In the verse above, He made them a promise. He promised that He would see them again. He promised to take them with Him to heaven, and that they would live together forever.

Answer these questions:

1. Name three people you know who you do not get to see very often.

   _____

   _____

   _____

2. When you see them, is it hard to say goodbye?

   _____

∂∽

3. With whom did Jesus spend His last night on earth?

_____

4. What promise did Jesus make to his disciples in the verse above?

_____

_____

Prayer: *Lord, thank you for promising to see us again. Help me be patient until I can see you face-to-face. Amen.*

LESSON 31a

HOME

George Washington spent time at Mount Vernon with Martha, her daughter, Nelly, and other family members. Most of all, he liked to ride across his land and see how the crops were growing, or being planted, and if the fences were mended. He took rides almost every day, even in the winter.

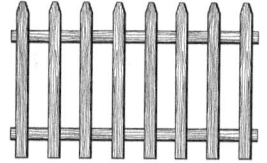

He had learned much about farming. He learned to rotate crops. That meant that he would plant one crop on a farm one year and a different crop, or no crop, the next year. This kept the land from being spent, and made the harvests bigger. He kept records of how the crops should be rotated each year so that workers would know which crops to plant on which farms.

Answer these questions about the story:

1. How did George Washington spend his time at Mount Vernon?

   _____

   _____

   _____

2. What do you like to do in your spare time?

   _____

   _____

   _____

3. What does it mean to "rotate" crops?

_____

_____

_____

4. Why did it help to rotate crops?

_____

_____

_____

5. Have you ever taught yourself to do something?

_____

If so, what?

_____

_____

_____

❧❧

LESSON 31b

HOME

Verse for the day: *for where your treasure is, there your heart will be also.*

Matthew 6:21 (NASB)

Remember the story you read about George Washington going home after being president?

Our home is usually a comfortable place for us to be. There are people there we know. We know how to behave there. Also, there are usually things at home we like to do, such as hobbies or games.

The verse above teaches us that our heart will be wherever our treasure is. Our treasures are the things dearest to us. Some children's treasures are toys or pets, but toys and pets go away. God wants the things dearest to us to last forever. Jesus' love for us and our love for Him and for others are some things which will last forever. Our treasures should be things like this.

Answer these questions:

1. What are some of your treasures?

   _____

   _____

   _____

2. Do you spend a lot of time thinking about these things?

   _____

3. Are these things that will last forever?

_____

4. What are some things we can have that will last forever?

_____

_____

_____

Prayer: _Lord, help me to spend time doing and thinking about things which will last forever. Amen._

LESSON 32a

DEATH

In the winter of 1799, George Washington got very sick. He sent for his doctor, but nothing the doctor did helped him get better. He told the doctor that he was going to die, but that he was not afraid. Later that night, George Washington died at home in his bed at Mount Vernon.

People all over the United States were sad. Government leaders all wore black to show that they were sad. The Speaker's chair, which sat in front of all the lawmakers, was also draped in black. Even in other countries, people were sad. The French put black flags in the streets. Even the British, who Washington had fought in the war, lowered their flags in respect. Washington was buried in a tomb at Mount Vernon.

Answer these questions about the story:

1. What year did George Washington die?

   _____

2. Turn back to *Lesson 1a* to see when George Washington was born.

   Can you figure out how old he was when he died?

   _____

3. What did the American government leaders do to show that they

   were sad?

   _____

   _____

   _____

✑✑

4. What did the British do?

_____

_____

5. Where was Washington buried?

_____

6. Why do you think people feel sad when someone they know dies?

_____

_____

_____

_____

⚘⚘

LESSON 32b

DEATH

> **Verse for the day:** *O DEATH, WHERE IS YOUR VICTORY? O DEATH, WHERE IS YOUR STING?*
>
> *I Corinthians 15:55 (NASB)*

Remember the story you read about George Washington's death?

It is very sad when people we know die. We know that we will not see them again on earth, and we will miss them. Sometimes we may even fear our own death.

Jesus had to face death, just like the rest of us. He died on a cross. But, in the end, Jesus defeated death. He rose again, and when He did, He gave us the same power to defeat death, too. This does not mean that we will not be sad when someone dies, or that we will live forever on the earth. But it does mean that we do not have to be afraid of death anymore.

Answer these questions:

1. What are some things that might hurt you?

   _____

   _____

   _____

2. Are you afraid of these things?

   _____

∽∝∽

3. What does the verse tell us we no longer have to be afraid of?

_____

4. Why don't we have to be afraid of death anymore?

_____

_____

Prayer: *Lord, thank you for defeating death. Help me to remember that I don't have to fear death anymore. Amen.*

LESSON 33a

A WILL

George Washington left a long will when he died. A will is something that tells people what to do with their belongings when they die. George Washington was very rich, and left a lot of land and money to Martha. He gave gifts to other members of his family too. He set aside a large amount of money to start a college.

At the time George Washington lived, many rich men owned slaves. George Washington owned more than a hundred slaves. The most important and well-known thing that George Washington did in his will is that he gave all the slaves their freedom. He even left money to help them make new lives for themselves. He made it very clear in his will that the slaves should never have to work for anyone as slaves again.

Answer these questions about the story:

1. What is a "will?"

_____

_____

_____

2. Why do you think George Washington wanted to start a college?

_____

_____

_____

❧❧

3. What did George Washington say should be done with the slaves?

_____

_____

_____

LESSON 33b

A WILL

Verse for the day: *So if the Son makes you free, you will be free indeed.*

John 8:36 (NASB)

Remember the story you read about George Washington freeing his slaves when he died?

In the time of George Washington, a slave had to work for his master. He could not decide what he would do on any day. He simply had to follow directions. Some freed slaves had the chance to go to college or start a business.

The verse above shows us that Jesus has given us freedom from sin. Under sin, we could only do wrong. Now, we have the freedom to do right if we want to, or we can continue to do wrong. It is our choice because we are free. God wants us to use our freedom to do good things.

Answer these questions:

1. What are some things your parents make you do?

_____

_____

_____

ৡৡ

2. Would you do those things even if your parents did not make you?

_____

Why?

_____

_____

3. What are some good things that you had the chance to do today but you didn't?

_____

_____

_____

Why didn't you do those things?

_____

_____

Prayer: *Lord, thank you for setting me free from sin. Help me to use my freedom to do good things. Amen.*

LESSON 34a

LEGACY

A legacy is something that someone leaves behind after they die that reminds people how important his life was.

Today, over 200 years after Washington's death, you will see many things that have taken Washington's name. Our nation's capital is Washington, D.C, which is named after him. There is also a state named Washington and at least three colleges bear his name. Many schools, hospitals, counties, and cities are named Washington.

Many people have been named after Washington, including famous people. George Washington Carver was a famous inventor. George Washington Lafayette was the son of Washington's friend, Lafayette. Washington Irving, who was also named after George Washington, was a famous author. One of Washington Irving's most famous books was a biography of George Washington.

All of these things are a part of George Washington's legacy. Since there are so many people and things named for him, we know he must have been very important.

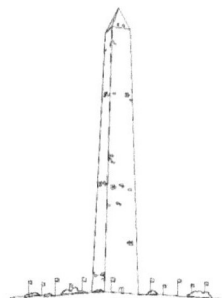

Answer these questions about the story:

1. Name three people who were named after George Washington?

_____

_____

_____

∾∾

2. Name two things (not people) that have been named after George Washington.

_____

_____

3. What is a "biography"?

_____

_____

4. Talk to your parents about the word "legacy". What does it mean to them?

_____

_____

_____

✺⌀✺

LESSON 34b

LEGACY

> **Verse for the day:** *I also say to you that you are Peter, and upon this rock I will build my church...*
>
> *Matthew 16:18 (NASB)*

Remember the story you read about George Washington's legacy?

Like Washington, Jesus left a very big legacy behind Him. In the verse above, we see that His Church is part of His legacy. The Church began with Peter and the disciples and continues with us today. In other words, you and I are part of Jesus' legacy! We are the way that other people can see that Jesus was here on earth and that He made a big difference in the world. They will know that He is real because He has made such a difference in our lives. It is a great responsibility to be a Christian and follow in the footsteps of Christ. Just as a statue of George Washington shows what Washington was like, we are statues of Christ and should show the world what Christ is like.

Answer these questions:

1. What is Jesus' legacy here on earth?

   _____

2. How has Jesus changed your life?

   _____

   _____

   _____

ふる

3. What can you do to show others what Jesus is like?

_____

_____

_____

4. How does it make you feel to be a part of Jesus' legacy?

_____

_____

_____

Prayer: *Lord, thank you for making me part of your legacy on earth. Help me to show others what you are truly like. Amen.*

⌐𝕤⌐𝕤